Run Win Impact

This book is a work of nonfiction. The author shares personal experiences and insights for educational and inspirational purposes. Individual results may vary. Readers are encouraged to seek professional guidance where appropriate.

Scripture quotations are taken from the New International Version (NIV), unless otherwise noted.

Published by Publisher Steps On Purpose Publish

ISBN: 978-1-972165-02-7
eBook ISBN: 978-1-972165-03-4

First Edition

Printed in the United States of America

Introduction

Most people are not stuck because they lack ability.

They are stuck because they lack direction.

They are moving, reacting, trying, surviving, adjusting, and doing their best to figure life out as they go. But movement without direction can still leave you exhausted, frustrated, and off course.

There are moments in life when you realize you were made for more.

Not more pressure.

Not more comparison.

Not more performance.

More purpose.

More clarity.

More alignment.

More intention in how you live and move forward.

This book was written for that moment.

Not as a quick fix.

Not as a motivational push that fades.

But as a guide to help you understand how to live with purpose in every step.

Too often, people move through life reacting.

Responding to circumstances.

Adjusting to pressure.

Comparing themselves to others.

Trying to figure things out as they go.

But you were not designed to drift.

You were designed to move with intention.

There is a race set before you.

A course that is yours to run.

A path that is not random, but designed.

This book is about learning how to run that race.

To run with clarity.

To run with consistency.

To run with purpose.

It is built around three ideas:

Run.

Win.

Impact.

Run is learning how to move with purpose and direction.

Win is understanding what success really looks like.

Impact is using what you have been given to make a difference.

This is not about perfection.

It is about alignment.

It is about taking responsibility for how you show up.

It is about making decisions that move you forward.

It is about staying consistent when things get difficult.

And it is about understanding that you are not doing this alone.

God has already placed purpose inside of you.

He has already begun a work in you.

Your role is not to create purpose.

Your role is to walk it out.

As you move through this book, you will be challenged.

You will be asked to reflect.

You will be asked to think differently.

You will be asked to take action.

Not all at once.

But step by step.

This is not about rushing.

It is about moving with intention.

Because direction matters more than speed.

The goal is not just to read this.

The goal is to live it.

To take what you learn and apply it.

To become more aware of how you think, how you respond, and how you move.

And ultimately, to run your race in a way that leads to something meaningful.

This is your race.

Run it with purpose.

Win through faithfulness.

Impact the world around you.

Who This Is For

This book was written for those who know they are capable of more but need direction to move forward.

Whether you are a student trying to find your path, a young adult navigating your next season, a mentor guiding others, or someone ready to live with greater intention—this framework is for you.

Some will read this for personal growth.
Others will use it to lead, teach, and develop those around them.

No matter where you are starting, the goal is the same:

To move with purpose.
To stay aligned.
To make an impact.

HOW TO USE THIS BOOK

This book is not meant to be read once and set aside.

It is meant to be lived.

Read through each chapter to understand the journey.

Then go back and slow down.

Reflect on what stands out.

Be honest about where you are.

Use the "Putting It Into Practice" section to take action.

Focus on one step at a time.

Not everything at once.

If you are working through this with others, use the Group Discussion Guide to create conversation, accountability, and growth.

This is not about perfection.

It is about progress.

Stay in your lane.
Stay in motion.
Stay aligned.

Run.
Win.
Impact.

THE FRAMEWORK

RUN • WIN • IMPACT

This book is built on a simple but powerful progression.

Not random movement.
Not reaction.
Not drifting.

But intentional living.

1. DESIGN

Before there was a decision, there was a design.

You were:

Known
Formed
Set apart
Appointed

Your life is not random.

Purpose existed before you were aware of it.

This is where most people lose clarity.
They try to discover purpose without understanding they were already designed for it.

2. DECISIONS

You are constantly choosing:

Will I agree with God or my insecurity?
Will I move with intention or react to circumstances?
Will I align with purpose or drift away from it?

Your decisions determine your direction.

Every step you take is reinforcing something.
Either alignment or drift.

3. DIRECTION

Direction is formed through consistent steps.

Small steps matter.
Daily choices matter.
Alignment matters.

You do not arrive by accident.
You arrive by direction.

This is where your race begins to take shape.
Not in one big moment, but in repeated ones.

4. DESTINY

Over time, your direction becomes your destiny.

Not in one moment.
But through a pattern of faithful steps.

What God designed begins to unfold as you walk it out.

This is not about rushing.
It is about staying aligned long enough to see it develop.

RUN • WIN • IMPACT

RUN
Move with purpose in every step.

WIN
Stay aligned with what you were designed to do.

IMPACT
Live in a way that transforms others, not just yourself.

You are not creating purpose.

You are walking out what was already designed.

Run your race.
Win through faithfulness.
Impact the world around you.

RUN: You Were Designed on Purpose

Before I ever understood purpose, I understood pressure.

Before I ever believed I had value, I felt the weight of being different.

I was born with a mark on my forehead, a port wine stain that made me stand out before I ever had a chance to fit in.

People did not have to know my name to notice me.

I was visible, but I did not feel valued.

They laughed.
They stared.
They talked.

Even some of the greatest have faced moments that could have defined them.

Michael Jordan, widely considered one of the greatest basketball players of all time, was cut from his high school varsity team.

Imagine that.

Not overlooked for a moment, but told you are not good enough.

For many people, that would have become their identity.

"I'm not good enough."
"I don't belong."
"This isn't for me."

But he made a different decision.

He did not let that moment define him.

He let it develop him.

He went back to work.

He trained.
He practiced.
He stayed committed.

What could have been a stopping point
became a starting point.

And the same question applies to all of us:

Will this moment define you,
or will it develop you?

Over time, what people said about me started shaping what I believed about myself.

I did not see purpose.
I saw a problem.

I did not see design.
I saw defect.

What I did not know then was this:

Before I was ever misunderstood,
I was already marked.

Not damaged.
Designed.

A diamond does not begin as something beautiful.

It starts buried, unseen, under pressure.

To the untrained eye, it looks like nothing special, just a rough stone surrounded by weight and dirt.

But what makes a diamond valuable is not how it starts.

It is what it contains.
And what it goes through.

Pressure does not destroy it.

Pressure reveals it.

Over time, that pressure shapes it.

It removes what does not belong.
It brings out what was always inside.

Not by accident.
By process.

Many people misunderstand their own lives in the same way.

Some think they are buried,
when they are actually being developed.

The greatest problem most people face is not a lack of ability.

It is a lack of identity and vision.

When you do not know who you are, you compare.

When you compare, you drift.

When you drift, you lose direction.

When you lose direction, you begin to live without intention.

Every step is either aligning you or drifting you.

As it says in the Bible, Proverbs 29:18:

"Where there is no vision, the people perish."

Another way to understand that is this:

Where there is no revelation,
people cast off restraint.

They run wild.
They live without direction.

Not because they are incapable.

But because they are unclear.

When there is no vision, there is no direction.
When there is no direction, there is no discipline.
When there is no discipline, there is no intentional movement.

That is how people drift.

Not all at once.

But step by step.

Most people see themselves through the wrong lens.

They see themselves through:

Pain
Past experiences
People's opinions
Present circumstances

But there is a better way to see yourself.

The Designer Lens asks one question:

What was God's original intent when He made me?

Not what happened to you.
Not what people said about you.
Not even what you have done.

But why were you created in the first place?

Because if you do not define your identity by design, you will define it by damage.

For years, I saw my mark as something that made me less.

Less confident.
Less accepted.
Less normal.

But what I did not realize was this:

The very thing I thought disqualified me
was part of what distinguished me.

It made me visible.
It made me memorable.
It shaped how I saw others who felt overlooked.
It developed a sensitivity I would not have had otherwise.

Over time, I began to understand:

What I thought was a flaw
was part of my formation.

Before you can run your race,
you have to see yourself correctly.

You are not an accident.
You are not a mistake.
You were created with intention.

There is something about you that stands out.

Something you may have questioned,
tried to hide,
or wished was different.

But that difference may be connected to your assignment.

What makes you different
may be what makes you impactful.

Pressure in your life is not always punishment.

Sometimes it is preparation.

What feels like weight
may be working on something within you,
shaping you,
refining you,
strengthening you.

You do not have to be like everyone else.

You do not have to follow someone else's path.

You have your own lane.
Your own pace.
Your own purpose.

Comparison will distract you
from what you were designed to do.

You cannot run your race
if you do not believe you have one.

You cannot run with purpose
if you do not understand who you are.

Reflect and Run

What have I believed about myself that came from people, not purpose?

What difference or mark have I been trying to hide?

Where in my life have I felt pressure, and what could it be producing?

Take a moment and shift your lens.

Ask yourself:

What was God's intent when He made me?

Then take one step on purpose.

Not to become something new,
but to uncover what has always been there.

You are not trying to become something you were never meant to be.

You are uncovering what has always been there.

You are not buried.

You are being built.

Run.

RUN: You Are Already Enough

One of the greatest traps people fall into
is trying to earn what God has already given.

They believe if they do enough,
become enough,
fix enough,
or prove enough,

then they will finally matter.

But grace interrupts that lie.

Grace says your worth was settled
before your performance ever began.

There was a time in my life
when I did not see myself that way.

I struggled with a deep sense of inferiority.

I compared myself constantly.

How they looked.
How they talked.
What they had.
Where they came from.

I measured my worth
by my performance,
my circumstances,
and how I stacked up against others.

And no matter what I did,

it never felt like enough.

Part of that struggle showed up
in how I communicated.

I had a speech impediment.

I used to stutter badly.

I struggled to pronounce certain words.

I even had to go to a speech pathologist
to try to work through it.

When I would speak, I would get stuck.

And when I got stuck,

people would laugh.

Every time that happened,
it reinforced something in me.

It made me feel smaller.
It made me question myself.
It made me pull back.

Eventually, I became hesitant to speak at all.

I began to fear using my voice.

Not because I did not have something to say,

but because I did not believe
I could say it the right way.

Before I understood my purpose,
before I understood my design,

I measured myself
by what I lacked
instead of who I was.

So I tried to adjust.

Tried to become more like other people.
Tried to fit into what I thought
would make me acceptable.

But the more I compared,

the more I lost myself.

I was trying to earn
something that had already been given.

As it says in the Bible, Ephesians 1:4:

"He chose us in Him before the creation of the world
to be holy and blameless in His sight."

Before there was performance,
there was selection.

Before there was effort,
there was identity.

Before there was striving,
there was design.

This changes everything.

Because if your worth was established
before you performed,

then your performance cannot be
the source of your worth.

Grace does not remove the need for growth.

Grace gives you the foundation
to grow from.

When you know your worth is secure,
something changes.

You stop running scared.
You stop chasing validation.
You stop measuring yourself
against other people's lanes.

You stop trying to prove
what has already been established.

Grace gives you stability.

Grace gives you confidence.

Grace gives you the courage
to keep going when the race gets heavy.

This is where many people struggle.

They are moving,

but they are moving from pressure,
not purpose.

They are running,

but they are running from insecurity,
not identity.

They are progressing,

but they are exhausted
because they are carrying something
they were never meant to carry.

Grace was never meant to be
the starting point you leave behind.

It is the foundation
you continue to stand on.

This is the difference
between striving and alignment.

Striving says,
"I have to become enough."

Grace says,
"You already are. Now walk it out."

Comparison is one of the fastest ways
to fall out of alignment.

Comparison pulls your focus
away from your design
and places it on someone else's assignment.

Comparison causes you to measure your life
by someone else's pace.

But you do not compare masterpieces.

You do not compete with originals.

God broke the mold
when He created you.

There is no one else
with your exact design.

No one else
with your exact calling.

No one else
with your exact assignment.

So comparison is not just unnecessary.

It is misalignment.

And misalignment will always lead
to frustration.

Because you cannot fully run your race
while trying to match someone else's pace.

Grace pulls you back into alignment.

Grace reminds you:

Your worth is not in question.
Your identity is not up for negotiation.
You are already chosen.
You are already known.
You are already set apart.

This is what allows you to run freely.

Not because everything is easy,

but because everything is settled.

When your worth is settled,
your movement becomes different.

You stop forcing.
You stop striving.
You stop overthinking every step.

You begin to move with clarity.

Winning is not about outperforming others.

Winning is about staying aligned
with who you were created to be.

Winning starts with knowing
you do not have to win approval.

This is what makes impact possible.

When you are no longer consumed
with proving yourself,

you are free to serve others.

When you are no longer focused
on validation,

you are able to add value.

When you are no longer chasing worth,

you are able to walk in purpose.

Grace does not make you passive.

Grace positions you properly.

It allows you to run with clarity.

It allows you to run with confidence.

It allows you to run
without carrying unnecessary weight.

You are not trying to earn your place.

You are learning how to walk in it.

This is how purpose is lived.

Not from pressure.
But from identity.

Not from fear.
But from confidence.

Not from striving.
But from grace.

Reflect and Run

Where am I trying to earn what has already been given?

Where has comparison pulled me out of alignment?

What would change if I truly believed
my worth was already established?

Recognize where you have been striving.

Replace striving with alignment.

Then take your next step
from a place of identity,
not insecurity.

You were never designed
to run a race trying to prove your worth.

You were designed
to run from it.

When your worth is settled,
your direction becomes clearer.

Win.

RUN: Purpose Shapes Your Direction

A lot of people are waiting for purpose
to show up in a big moment.

They are looking for a clear sign.
A major opportunity.
A defining breakthrough.

They believe purpose is something you arrive at.

But purpose is not something you stumble into.

It is something you walk in.

Purpose is not found in big moments.

It is built in faithful steps.

There was a season in my life
where I was moving, but I was not clear.

I was doing things.
Showing up.
Making decisions.

But I was not always aligned.

Some decisions were based on pressure.
Some were based on comparison.
Some were based on what I thought I was supposed to do.

And when you live like that, something subtle happens.

You begin to drift.

Not all at once.
But slowly.

Quietly.
Without realizing it.

There was a season where I was moving, but I was not aligned.

I came into Upward Bound as a freshman carrying more than I knew how to handle.

Low self-esteem.
Inferiority.
Grief from losing my mother.
Pain from a father who was not present.

All of that was sitting beneath the surface.

One day in class, the teacher called me to the board to solve a problem.

I already did not feel confident.
I already questioned myself.

I got the problem wrong.

And in that moment, it was not just about the answer.

It felt like confirmation of everything I already believed about myself.

That I was not good enough.
That I did not belong.
That I could not measure up.

I did not say much, but my response showed it.

My frustration.
My anger.
My shame.

The teacher walked out of the room and went to the director's office.

I remember hearing the words:

"Steven Robertson, I want him out of the program."

Just like that.

One moment.
One response.
One decision.

But what I did not understand then was this:

That moment was not the problem.

It revealed what was already going on inside of me.

I was reacting, not responding.

Moving, but not aligned.

Dr. Lowery called me into his office.

He looked at me and said, "Mr. Robertson, I expect more out of you than this."

No one had ever spoken to me like that.

He held me accountable.

But he also saw something in me that I did not see in myself.

That moment forced me to slow down.

Not just in what I was doing.

But in how I was living.

Over time, something began to shift.

Not overnight.
Not in one big moment.

But in small decisions.

I started working on myself.

My attitude.
My response.
My discipline.
My focus.

I began to align my behavior with what was expected of me.

Step by step.
Choice by choice.

Years later, that same teacher came back.

But this time, she was not trying to remove me.

She was leading the program.

And I was no longer the same person.

I had grown.
I had aligned.
I had changed.

I graduated from Upward Bound.
Graduated from high school.
Was accepted into Marquette University.

And later, I came back to work in the very program that once questioned if I belonged.

Looking back, I understand something clearly now.

I did not drift because of one big decision.

I drifted because I was not aligned internally.

And I did not change in one moment.

I changed through small, consistent decisions
to align my life differently.

As it says in 1 Corinthians 9:26:

"Therefore I do not run like someone running aimlessly;
I do not fight like a boxer beating the air."

There is a difference between movement and direction.

You can be busy and still be off course.
You can be active and still be aimless.
You can be doing a lot
and still not be moving toward what matters.

Purpose gives your steps direction.

It aligns your decisions.

It shapes how you move.

Without purpose, you react.
With purpose, you respond.

Without purpose, you drift.
With purpose, you decide.

RECOGNIZING DRIFT IN REAL TIME

People do not drift because they do not care.

They drift because they do not notice.

Drift rarely shows up as something obvious.

It shows up in small, everyday decisions.

It looks like:

Saying yes when you should say no
Avoiding a decision you know you need to make
Letting how you feel override what you know
Choosing comfort over alignment
Staying busy instead of being intentional

Drift is subtle.

That is why it is dangerous.

If you want to stay aligned,
you have to learn to recognize drift early.

Ask yourself in real time:

Am I deciding from purpose or pressure?
Am I avoiding something I need to face?
Is this moving me forward or just keeping me busy?

Drift is not stopped by good intentions.

It is stopped by awareness and correction.

This is how Steps On Purpose works.

It is not built in one moment.

It is built in daily decisions.

Every step you take
is either aligning you
or drifting you.

There is no neutral.

Every choice carries direction.

Every response carries weight.

Every decision moves you somewhere.

There was a commercial flight in 1983
that drifted slightly off its intended course.

It did not happen all at once.

It started with a small deviation.
Just a few degrees off.

Over time, that small misalignment
carried the aircraft into restricted airspace
it was never meant to enter.

The flight ended in tragedy.

Not because of one major decision.

But because of a small, uncorrected shift in direction.

That is how life works.

You do not lose direction all at once.

You drift.

Small compromises.
Small distractions.
Small misalignments.

Over time, those small shifts take you somewhere
you never intended to go.

Before I understood this,
I thought purpose was something I needed to find.

But what I began to realize was this:

Purpose was already present.

I just needed to align my steps with it.

And that meant paying attention
to the small decisions.

What I said yes to.
What I said no to.
How I responded when things did not go my way.
How I handled pressure.
How I handled distraction.

Because direction is not decided in big moments.

It is shaped in small ones.

Purpose is direction.

Purpose is not just what you do.

It is how you move.

It shows up in your decisions.
Your discipline.
Your consistency.

If your steps are not aligned,
your direction will not be either.

Alignment is daily.

You do not align once.

You align daily.

Through choices.
Through habits.
Through responses.

Every day is an opportunity
to move closer
or drift further.

Small steps compound.

You do not need a big moment to walk in purpose.

You need consistent movement.

The small decisions you make today
shape the direction you live tomorrow.

This is what it means to run.

Run is not about speed.

Run is about direction.

Run is choosing alignment over drift.

Run is making decisions that move you forward,
even when they feel small.

Reflect and Run

Where in my life am I slowly drifting without realizing it?

What small decisions today are shaping my long term direction?

What is one adjustment I need to make now
before it becomes a bigger issue later?

Pause. Get honest. Then take the next step on purpose.

Purpose is not found in big moments.

It is built in faithful steps.

Direction is not decided in big moments.
It is shaped in small ones.

Run.

RUN: Your Race

One of the fastest ways to lose direction
is to start running someone else's race.

It does not happen all at once.

It happens quietly.

You look around.
You compare.
You measure your progress
against someone else's pace.

And before you realize it,
you are no longer running with purpose.

You are reacting.

As it says in Hebrews 12:1:

"Let us run with perseverance the race marked out for us."

There is a race marked out for you.

And it is set before you to run.

Not a general race.
Not a shared race.

A specific one.

Your pace.
Your path.
Your assignment.

And the moment you step outside of that,
confusion begins.

There was a time in my life when comparison
was not just something I struggled with.

It was how I saw myself.

I grew up with an inferiority complex.

I would look at other people
and immediately measure myself against them.

Their ability.
Their confidence.
Their performance.

And every time I did,
I came up second.

I came up lacking.

I came up feeling like I was not enough.

It did not matter what I was doing.

If someone else looked stronger,
smarter, or further ahead,
I would discount myself.

That is what comparison does.

It does not just distort how you see others.

It distorts how you see yourself.

The Bible says in 2 Corinthians 10:12
that when we compare ourselves with one another,
we are not wise.

Because comparison is based on the wrong standard.

You are not called to measure your life
against someone else's.

You are called to run your race.

I remember a time when I was on a track team and was asked to run the quarter mile.

One full lap.
All out.

I had never run it before.

No one explained how to pace it.
No one told me what to expect.

The coach simply asked me to run it.

And I said yes.

The gun went off.

I took off fast.

I was running hard.
Passing people.
Feeling strong.

Everything in me said I was doing it right.

But coming out of that curve,
something changed.

I was still moving.
Still pumping my arms.
Still driving my legs.

But it felt like I hit a wall.

Like something jumped on my back.

My body was still going,
but it was not responding the same way.

And in that moment, it was not just physical.

It was mental.

My thoughts started racing:

Did I start too fast?
Did I misjudge this race?
Why does this feel harder than expected?
Am I about to lose this?

Every step felt heavier.

Every second felt longer.

And one by one,
people started passing me.

Little by little.
Step by step.

I could see them moving ahead.

And I could feel myself fading.

And in that moment, something deeper hit me.

I was not just losing ground.

I was losing confidence.

And when confidence drops,
everything feels harder.

Your legs feel heavier.
Your breathing tightens.
Your focus begins to break.

For a moment,
quitting felt like the easiest option.

It would have been easy to slow down.
Easy to step off.
Easy to tell myself I was not built for this.

But something in me said:

Finish.

Not fast.
Not perfect.

Just finish.

Even if the pace changed,
I was not going to quit.

So I kept moving.

Step by step.
Stride by stride.

I finished the race.

And I learned something that day.

I did not lose that race at the end.

I lost it in how I started.

There is something else I learned about running that day.

When you run track, they teach you to keep your eyes forward.

Not to the left.
Not to the right.

Because the moment you start looking sideways,
looking at who is next to you,
looking at how fast they are moving,
looking at how they are running their race,
you lose focus.

You break your rhythm.

And even if it is subtle,
you begin to drift.

Life works the same way.

The moment you start looking around,
comparing yourself to others,
measuring your pace against someone else's,
you lose focus.

You lose rhythm.

And without realizing it,
you begin to drift.

Not because you stopped running,
but because you stopped focusing.

You cannot run your race clearly
while watching someone else's.

Comparison does not just distract you.
It misaligns you.

Running fast
is not the same as running right.

You can start strong
and still struggle
if you do not understand your race.

Everything began to change for me
when I stopped looking sideways
and started focusing forward.

When I realized:

I do not need what they have
to run what I was given.

I need to develop
what is already in me.

That is when my confidence began to shift.

Not because I became better than someone else,
but because I became aligned with myself.

Running your race requires awareness.

It requires discipline.

It requires focus.

It requires you to stay committed
to what God has given you,
not what He has given someone else.

Because the moment you measure your race
against someone else's,
you lose your rhythm.

You lose your focus.

And without realizing it,
you begin to drift.

RESETTING WHEN COMPARISON HITS

Comparison does not just happen.

It is triggered.

You see someone ahead of you.
You scroll past someone's success.
You hear about someone moving faster than you.

And in a moment, your focus shifts.

When that happens, pause.

Ask yourself:

What has God actually called me to do?
What season am I in right now?
What step is mine to take next?

Take your next on purpose step immediately.

Then refocus.

Comparison pulls your eyes outward.

Purpose pulls your focus inward.

The moment you shift your focus
back to your lane,
your clarity returns.

Your pace stabilizes.

Your confidence rebuilds.

Everyone you see
is not running the same distance.

Everyone you see
is not carrying the same assignment.

Everyone you see
is not in the same season.

Some are starting.
Some are building.
Some are finishing.

If you compare your beginning
to someone else's middle,
or your process
to someone else's outcome,
you will always feel behind.

Not because you are off,
but because you are looking
in the wrong direction.

Your responsibility
is not to run their race.

Your responsibility
is to run the race set before you.

There will be moments
where your pace slows down.

Moments where it feels heavier than expected.

Moments where you question
if you are still moving forward.

But pace does not determine purpose.

Faithfulness does.

Consistency does.

Endurance does.

This is what it means to run.

Run is not about speed.

Run is about staying in your lane.

Run is about maintaining focus
when distractions are everywhere.

Run is about continuing forward
even when the pace changes.

This is how you win.

You do not win your race
by being the fastest.

You win your race
by staying in it.

By staying focused.
By staying aligned.
By refusing to quit
when it gets hard.

Winning is not about outperforming others.

Winning is about finishing
what you were given to run.

This is where impact is formed.

Impact is built through faithfulness.

Impact is built through consistency.

Impact is built by people
who stay in their lane long enough
to make a difference.

Your race is lost
the moment you start running someone else's.

Reflect and Run

Where in my life am I comparing instead of focusing?

Where has comparison started affecting my confidence?

What has been pulling my attention away from my assignment?

What does it look like for me to stay in my lane this week?

Check your focus.

Realign your direction.

Then take your next step
and stay in your lane.

Run.

WIN: Discipline Sustains the Race

Running starts with direction.
Winning is sustained through discipline.

Motivation can start a race.

But it cannot sustain it.

There will be days you feel energized.
Days you feel focused.
Days everything seems clear.

But there will also be days
when none of that is present.

Days you do not feel like showing up.
Days progress feels slow.
Days the weight of consistency
feels heavier than the excitement of beginning.

That is where discipline matters.

I remember a defining moment in my life
when I had to choose
between what I wanted
and what was right.

I was in my third year at Marquette University.

Only three semesters away from graduating.

After everything I had come through,
I was on the verge of becoming
the first in my family to graduate from college.

But something shifted in me.

I developed a hunger for God.
A desire to grow.
A desire to pursue purpose at a deeper level.

And I became convinced
that I needed to leave immediately
and go to Bible college.

It felt right.
It felt urgent.
It felt like the next step.

So I went to my pastor,
Bishop Jonathan Saffold Sr.,
a man I respected and trusted.

I explained everything.
What I felt.
What I wanted.
What I believed I needed to do.

I also knew that I needed his recommendation
as part of the admission process to transfer.

And I asked for his recommendation.

He looked at me and asked one question:

How many semesters do you have left?

I told him, Three.

And without hesitation, he said:

Absolutely not.

That was not the answer I expected.

It made me angry.

I remember picking up rocks
and throwing them one by one
as he continued to speak.

The more he talked,
the more frustrated I became.

Because what he was telling me
was not what I wanted to hear.

He told me to finish.

He told me discipline mattered.

He told me that when I completed
what I started,
then I would have his full support.

In that moment, I had a choice:

Follow what I felt.
Or submit to what I knew was right.

I wanted to leave.

But I stayed.

And staying was not easy.

It required discipline.
It required consistency.
It required me to keep showing up
when I felt pulled in another direction.

But I finished.

Years later, I saw that same principle
play out in a completely different way.

I was riding in the car with my son.

He was young, about three or four years old.

We were talking about discipline.

I was explaining to him
the importance of training
and doing what is right.

I told him that as a father,
God would hold me accountable
if I did not train him
in the way he should go.

He looked at me and said:

So God will get you
if you do not train me?

I said, Yes, son.

God gives parents responsibility.

And I would be accountable
if I did not train you the right way.

We parked the car
and started walking toward church.

Some neighbors were outside,
sitting on their porch.

And out of nowhere,
he started yelling at the top of his voice:

God! God!
Daddy not training me!
Daddy not training me!

He said it again, loud,
like he was trying to get me in trouble.

In that moment, I had to respond quickly.

So I asked him:

Are you saying you want more training?
More lessons?
More discipline than what you are getting right now?

He did not hesitate.

No, no, no.

God, Daddy training me.
Daddy training me.

In that moment, I realized something.

Discipline is not always comfortable.

But it is always necessary.

And more than that,
discipline is not just personal.

It is generational.

What you practice, others will see.

What you model, others will follow.

Looking back now,
I understand something
I could not fully see then.

That decision to stay and finish
did not just impact me.

It shaped how I lead my family.
It shaped how I teach.
It shaped how I live.

Because discipline will take you
where motivation cannot.

As it says in the Bible, 1 Corinthians 9:24 to 25:

Do you not know that in a race all the runners run, but only one gets the prize? Run in such a way as to get the prize. Everyone who competes in the games goes into strict training.

Discipline is not intensity in a moment.

It is consistency over time.

It is showing up when it is inconvenient.
It is continuing when it is uncomfortable.
It is staying committed
when the emotion is no longer there.

A lot of people rely on motivation.

But motivation is temporary.

It rises and falls.
It comes and goes.

If your life is built on motivation,
your progress will always be inconsistent.

Discipline builds
what motivation cannot sustain.

Every step you repeat
is either aligning you
or drifting you.

There is an illustration of a stonecutter.

He strikes a rock with his hammer.

Nothing happens.

He strikes it again.

Still nothing.

He strikes it a hundred times,
and the rock does not appear to move.

Then, on the next strike,
the rock splits in two.

It was not the final strike alone
that broke the stone.

It was every strike before it.

Each one mattered,
even when no progress was visible.

That is how discipline works.

Progress is often invisible
before it becomes undeniable.

Discipline is not just what you do.

It is what you repeat.

Your habits shape your direction.

Your routines shape your outcomes.

Your consistency shapes your future.

You do not need to feel ready.

You need to be consistent.

You do not need perfect conditions.

You need repeated commitment.

You do not need constant motivation.

You need discipline.

Discipline carries you
when motivation cannot.

Reflect and Run

What am I currently relying on
that cannot sustain where I am trying to go?

Where am I being inconsistent
in a way that is quietly costing me more than I realize?

What would change
if I committed to showing up the same way,
regardless of how I feel?

Recognize where you have been inconsistent.

Replace inconsistency with commitment.

Then take your next step
and repeat it.

Win.

WIN: Master Your Inner Voice

Discipline helps you show up.
But what you believe determines how you show up.

Not every battle you face is external.

Some of the hardest battles you will fight are internal.

They do not come from what is happening around you.

They come from what is happening within you.

Your thoughts.
Your perspective.
Your internal voice.

There are moments in life where what you are facing begins to feel bigger than what you can handle.

Situations stack up.
Pressure builds.
Emotions intensify.

And if you are not careful, something begins to happen.

You start to magnify the problem.

What was once manageable begins to feel overwhelming.
What was once temporary begins to feel permanent.
What was once a challenge begins to feel like a conclusion.

This is how internal battles begin.

Not all at once.
But gradually.

Thought by thought.
Moment by moment.

Until what you are thinking starts to shape what you believe.

And what you believe starts to shape how you see yourself.

And how you see yourself begins to shape how you live.

I remember having to learn this lesson in a very real way.

There were seasons in my life where the external challenge was not the hardest part.

The hardest part was what I was saying to myself about it.

The internal conversation.
The doubt.
The second guessing.
The questions that did not always have answers.

Am I really capable of this?
What if I fail?
What if I am not enough?

Those thoughts did not come all at once.

They showed up over time.

And if left unchecked, they started to sound like truth.

But just because a thought is present does not mean it is true.

That was a shift I had to make.

I had to learn how to challenge my own thinking.

Because if you do not confront your internal voice, it will begin to control your direction.

As it says in the Bible, 2 Corinthians 10:5:

"Take every thought captive
to the obedience of Christ."

That means not every thought gets agreement.

Some thoughts must be challenged.
Some thoughts must be replaced.
Some thoughts must be rejected.

Because your thoughts are not neutral.

They are shaping something.

They are shaping your confidence.
They are shaping your perspective.
They are shaping your decisions.

And over time, they are shaping your life.

There were moments where I had to speak differently before I felt differently.

Moments where I had to say:

I am not what I have been through.
I am not what people said about me.
I am not limited by what I feel right now.

Even when I did not fully believe it.

Because what you consistently say has a way of shaping what you eventually believe.

And what you believe has a way of shaping how you show up.

This is why your inner voice matters.

If your internal voice is filled with doubt, you will hesitate.
If it is filled with fear, you will hold back.
If it is filled with comparison, you will question your place.

But if your internal voice is grounded in truth, you will move with clarity.
You will move with confidence.
You will move with alignment.

Every thought you agree with
is either aligning you
or drifting you.

Winning is not just about what you do externally.

It is about what you believe internally.

Because you cannot consistently act in a way that contradicts what you believe.

Eventually, your belief system will pull your behavior back into alignment.

This is why mastering your inner voice is essential.

It is not about pretending everything is okay.

It is about choosing what is true over what is loud.

You may not control every thought that comes to your mind.

But you do control which ones you agree with.

That is where discipline meets belief.

Discipline helps you show up.
Belief determines how you show up.

And when both are aligned, your movement becomes powerful.

Reflect and Run

What thoughts have I been agreeing with that are not aligned with truth?

Where have I allowed my internal voice to go unchallenged?

What truth do I need to begin speaking, even if I do not fully feel it yet?

Get honest about what you have been agreeing with.

Replace it with truth.

Then take your next step on purpose.

Win.

WIN: Shape Your Environment

Discipline shapes your actions.
But your environment shapes what becomes natural.

You are always being shaped.

Every environment you are in.
Every voice you listen to.
Every habit you repeat.
Every standard you accept.

Something is forming you.

The question is not whether you are being shaped.

The question is what is shaping you.

As it says in the Bible, Proverbs 13:20:

Walk with the wise and become wise,
for a companion of fools suffers harm.

Who you walk with matters.

What you allow around you matters.

What you repeatedly expose yourself to matters.

Because over time,
what surrounds you begins to influence you.

And what influences you begins to shape you.

And what shapes you eventually steers you.

Most people underestimate the power of environment.

They think their decisions are independent.

They think their mindset is self contained.

They think their habits are purely personal.

But environment is always speaking.

Even when you are not paying attention.
Even when you are not aware.

It is shaping what you normalize.

It is shaping what you tolerate.

It is shaping what you believe is possible.

Think about it this way.

If you place a seed in healthy soil,
it has the opportunity to grow.

If you place that same seed in poor soil,
its growth is limited.

The seed did not change.

The environment did.

And the outcome followed the environment.

The same is true in your life.

Your potential may be strong.
Your calling may be real.
Your ability may be present.

But if your environment does not support growth,
it will limit what develops.

Environment does not just affect comfort.

It affects capacity.

Now this is important to understand.

This does not mean
you cannot grow in a difficult environment.

People do it every day.

There are individuals
who come from challenging situations,
limited resources,
and environments that were not designed for growth,
and they still rise.

So this is not about limitation.

It is about influence.

Environment does not decide your outcome.

But it does affect your development.

It can make growth more difficult.

It can require more discipline.
More awareness.
More resilience.

Because when your environment is not supporting your growth,
you have to supply what is missing.

You have to think differently
when everything around you thinks small.

You have to stay focused
when everything around you is distracting.

You have to stay disciplined
when everything around you is inconsistent.

That takes strength.

That takes intention.

That takes ownership.

And many people have done it.

But it is important to be honest.

It is harder to grow
in an environment that is working against you
than in one that is working with you.

That is why awareness matters.

Because once you recognize
what is influencing you,
you can begin to make adjustments.

You can change what you expose yourself to.

You can shift what you listen to.

You can become more intentional
about what shapes your thinking.

And over time,
you can begin to reshape your environment
even if you did not choose where you started.

Your environment may influence your beginning.

But it does not have the final say in your direction.

Think about the difference
between a thermostat and a thermometer.

A thermometer only reflects
the temperature of the room.

If the room is cold, it reads cold.
If the room is hot, it reads hot.

It does not change anything.

It only responds.

A thermostat is different.

A thermostat sets the temperature.

It does not adjust to the environment.

It influences it.

Many people live like thermometers.

They adjust to whatever is around them.

If the environment is negative,
they become negative.

If the standard is low,
they lower their standard.

If the energy is off,
they follow it.

They are being shaped
without realizing it.

But when you become aware,
you have a choice.

You can continue to reflect your environment.

Or you can begin to influence it.

You can raise your standard.

You can shift your focus.

You can decide what you allow to shape you.

Because while environment influences you,
it does not have to control you.

At its core, environment is influence.

The people around you are influencing you.

The voices you listen to are influencing you.

The standards you accept are influencing you.

That is why leadership matters.

Leadership is influence.

Nothing more.
Nothing less.

Every person you follow is shaping something in you.

How they think.
How they respond.
What they value.

And whether you realize it or not,
you are doing the same for others.

Someone is watching how you move.

Someone is learning from how you respond.

Someone is being influenced
by what you tolerate
and what you prioritize.

So this is not just about
what is shaping you.

It is also about
what is flowing through you.

You are not just a product of your environment.

You are becoming a contributor to it.

That means you have responsibility.

Responsibility to be intentional
about what you allow to influence you.

And responsibility to be aware
of how your life is influencing others.

There was a time
when I noticed how much
the people around me
were influencing my thinking.

The conversations I was part of.

The attitudes I was exposed to.

The expectations that were being set.

It was shaping how I saw myself.

It was shaping how I approached opportunities.

It was shaping what I believed I could or could not do.

And the more I stayed in that environment,
the more normal it became.

Nothing felt off.

Nothing felt wrong.

But over time,
I realized I was being shaped
in a direction I did not intend.

Not because of one major decision.

But because I stayed in a space
that was quietly influencing me.

That is how environment works.

It does not always force you.

It forms you.

It shapes your thinking
before it shapes your actions.

And once your thinking is shaped,
your direction follows.

You do not drift into a new direction randomly.

You are influenced into it consistently.

This is where Steps On Purpose becomes critical.

Your steps are not just shaped
by your decisions.

They are shaped by your environment.

And if your environment is misaligned,
your steps will eventually follow.

Every influence you allow
is either aligning you
or drifting you.

That is why you have to be intentional
about what you allow around you.

Who is speaking into your life?

What voices are you listening to?

What conversations are shaping your perspective?

What standards are being reinforced around you?

These things matter more than most people realize.

Because you will eventually move
in the direction
of what you are consistently exposed to.

If you are surrounded by limitation,
you will begin to think small.

If you are surrounded by negativity,
you will begin to expect less.

If you are surrounded by growth,
you will begin to expand.

If you are surrounded by discipline,
you will begin to sharpen.

Environment does not guarantee success.

But it strongly influences direction.

And if you are not intentional,
it will shape you by default.

You cannot always control every environment you are in.

But you can control what you allow to influence you.

You can choose what you listen to.

You can choose what you engage.

You can choose what you internalize.

And those choices
will shape who you become.

WHAT YOU TOLERATE BECOMES YOUR STANDARD

One of the most subtle ways
environment shapes you
is through what you tolerate.

What you accept repeatedly
becomes normal.

What becomes normal
eventually becomes expected.

And what is expected
begins to define your standard.

If you tolerate inconsistency,
it becomes your pattern.

If you tolerate negativity,
it becomes your mindset.

If you tolerate distraction,
it becomes your habit.

Standards are not set in big moments.

They are set in repeated allowances.

That is why you have to raise your awareness.

You have to pay attention
to what is influencing you.

You have to be honest
about what is shaping your thinking.

Because once you see it,
you can begin to change it.

And once you change it,
your direction can shift.

This is what it means to win.

Winning is not just about discipline.

It is about alignment.

It is about surrounding yourself
with what supports your growth.

And this is what creates impact.

When your environment supports your purpose,
your growth becomes sustainable.

And sustainable growth
creates lasting influence.

You are not only shaped by your decisions.

You are shaped by what you allow
to influence them.

Reflect and Run

What in my environment is quietly shaping me
in a direction I do not want?

What am I consistently exposed to
that is influencing how I think and act?

What is one change I need to make
to create an environment
that supports who I am becoming?

Pause.

Get honest.

Then take your next step on purpose.

Win.

WIN: Run Through the Finish

There comes a point in every race
where starting is no longer the focus.

The middle has passed.
The end is in sight.
And everything in you feels the weight
of what it takes to finish.

This is where races are decided.

Not at the beginning.
Not when energy is high
and motivation is strong.

But in the stretch.

The moment where your body feels it.
Your mind feels it.
Your pace wants to slow.
Your focus begins to drift.

This is where you have to decide.

Will you ease up,
or will you run through the finish?

There was a moment in the 1992 Olympics
that captured what it truly means to finish.

A runner named Derek Redmond
was competing in the 400 meter semifinal.

He had trained for years.
He was prepared.
He was ready.

The race started,
and everything looked strong.

But halfway through, something went wrong.

His hamstring tore.

In an instant, everything changed.

He pulled up in visible pain.
The race continued without him.
Runners passed.
The moment was gone.

Most people would have stopped.

Most people would have accepted
that it was over.

But he did something different.

He got back up.

In pain, he began to move forward.

Step by step.
Limping.
Struggling.
But refusing to stop.

Then something even more powerful happened.

His father broke through security
and came onto the track.

He wrapped his arm around him.

And together, they moved forward.

Slowly.
Painfully.
But intentionally.

They crossed the finish line.

Not first.
Not fast.

But finished.

That moment was not about winning.

It was about refusing to quit.

That is what it looks like
to run through the finish.

In your life, you will face moments
where finishing feels harder than starting.

Moments where the energy is gone.
Where the results are not immediate.
Where the cost of continuing
feels higher than the reward.

That is where your decision matters most.

Running through the finish
is not about how you feel.

It is about what you choose.

You choose to keep going
when everything in you wants to slow down.

You choose to stay focused
when distractions increase.

You choose to give what you have left
instead of holding back.

That is where discipline becomes visible.

Not in perfect conditions.

But in pressure.

Not when it is easy.

But when it is difficult.

Everyone can start.

Fewer people stay.

Even fewer people finish strong.

Running through the finish
means you do not ease up
in the moment that matters most.

You lean in.

You lock in.

You give everything you have left.

This is where your KICK shows up.

Keep going.
Increase focus.
Commit fully.
Kick with what is left.

Every step in the stretch
is either aligning you
or drifting you.

This is not about being perfect.

It is about being intentional.

It is about finishing the race
you were given to run.

Because how you finish
matters.

Reflect and Run

Where in my life am I tempted to ease up before the finish?

What does my KICK look like in this season?

What is one area where I need to increase focus and commit fully?

Pause. Get honest.
Then take your next on purpose step.

Win.

IMPACT: Let Your Light Be Seen

You were never meant to hide
what God placed inside of you.

Not your faith.

Not your growth.

Not your transformation.

What God is doing in your life
is not just for you.

It is meant to be seen.

It is meant to be lived.

It is meant to influence others.

As it says in the Bible, Matthew 5:16:

Let your light so shine before others,
that they may see your good works
and glorify your Father in heaven.

Light does not have to announce itself.

It simply shows up.

And when it does,
it changes the environment.

Darkness does not overcome light.

Light removes darkness.

Notice what the Scripture says.

Let your light so shine.

It does not just say
let your light shine.

It says
let your light so shine.

That word matters.

It is describing how your light shows up.

Not casual.
Not occasional.
Not hidden.

Intentional.
Visible.
Consistent.

In this manner.
In this way.
In a way that produces something.

Your light is not just meant to exist.

It is meant to be expressed.

It is meant to show up
in how you live.

But it goes deeper.

Your light does not come
from the outside.

It comes from within.

It comes from your soul.

From who you are
on the inside.

From your character.
From your convictions.
From your consistency.
From what God has done in you.

That means your light
is not performance.

It is not something you turn on
when people are watching.

It is not something you manufacture.

It is something that flows.

It flows out of your life.

It flows out of your growth.

It flows out of your transformation.

So when your light so shines,
it is not shallow.

It is not forced.

It is not temporary.

It is real.

It is steady.

It is rooted.

It shows up in how you respond under pressure.

How you treat people
when it is inconvenient.

How you carry yourself
when no one is watching.

That is what it means
to let your light so shine.

Not just visible.

But authentic.

Not just seen.

But real.

Not just external.

But flowing from within.

Light does more
than make things visible.

Light gives direction.

When something is dark,
you cannot see clearly.

You cannot tell where you are going.

You cannot see what is in front of you.

You move carefully.

Uncertain.

Hesitant.

But when light shows up,
everything changes.

The path becomes clearer.

The next step becomes visible.

What once felt uncertain
begins to make sense.

This is what impact looks like.

When your light is visible in your life,
it first brings clarity to you.

It helps you see your path.

It helps you walk with direction.

It helps you move with intention.

And as that light continues to shine,
it does not stop with you.

It begins to provide light
and guidance for others.

Your light can illuminate your path
and someone else's.

It can help you move forward with clarity
while helping someone else see
what is possible.

Your light should help
brighten someone else's path.

It should help them see
where they could not see before.

It should help them take a step
they were unsure about.

Your life can light up
someone else's life.

Not because you are perfect.

But because you are real.

Because you kept going.

Because you did not quit.

Because you grew.

And when people see that,
it gives them strength.

It gives them perspective.

It gives them hope.

If you made it through,
maybe I can too.

If you survived it,
maybe I can survive it.

If you are growing,
maybe I am not stuck.

That is what light does.

It does not just shine.

It strengthens.

There was a moment
that captured this clearly
on a public stage.

In 2023,
Damar Hamlin
collapsed on the field
during a nationally televised game.

In that moment,
everything stopped.

Players gathered.

Coaches surrounded.

Fans watched in silence.

And something happened
that you do not always see
in public spaces.

People began to pray.

Not privately.

Not quietly.

Openly.

But what mattered just as much
was what happened after.

How he responded.

How he carried himself.

How he pointed beyond himself.

His life became a signal.

Not just of survival.

But of perspective.

Of gratitude.

Of something bigger than the moment.

And that light reached people.

Not just because of what happened to him.

But because of how he lived after it.

That is impact.

Not just what you go through.

But how you come through it.

There is an important balance in this.

You are not called to hide your life.

But you are also not called
to take the credit for it.

Scripture says
to let your light shine
so that people may see your good works
and glorify your Father in heaven.

That means your life
should produce something visible.

Growth should be seen.

Change should be seen.

Consistency should be seen.

There should be evidence
that something is happening
in your life.

But the goal
is not for people to stop at you.

The goal
is for them to see beyond you.

You are not the source.

You are the reflection.

When people see your life,
they should not just say,
Look at them.

They should begin to recognize,

Something is working in them.

Something real.

Something steady.

Something different.

And that points them to God.

You are not trying to get the glory.

You are giving it.

There is another layer to this.

Scripture tells us
that we are saved by grace through faith.

Not of ourselves.

Not of works.

So that no one can boast.

That means your life
is not built on what you have earned.

It is built on what you have received.

But it does not stop there.

Because it also says
that we are God's workmanship.

Created in Christ Jesus
for good works.

You are not saved by works.

But you are saved for them.

Your identity
is not built on performance.

But your life
should still produce evidence.

Grace is the foundation.

Good works are the expression.

You do not live this way
to earn anything.

You live this way
because something
has already been given to you.

So your life should reflect that.

Not perfectly.

But genuinely.

When people see your life,
they should not see someone
trying to prove themselves.

They should see someone
who has been changed.

Someone who is growing.

Someone who is living out
what has been placed inside of them.

And that brings it back to light.

Your light is not self produced.

It is the result
of what God has done in you.

So when your light shines,
it is not about you getting the credit.

It is about God
being revealed through you.

You are not trying to earn the light.

You are revealing it.

And when people see your life
and recognize something real,
something consistent,
something transformed,

they do not just see you.

They begin to glorify God.

This is what it means to run.

Run is not just about movement.

Run is about expression.

Run is not proving who you are.

Run is revealing
who you have become.

This is how you win.

Winning is not just internal.

Winning becomes visible.

Winning shows up
in how you live,
how you respond,
and how you carry
what God has placed inside of you.

And this is what creates impact.

Impact happens
when what is in you
reaches beyond you.

When your life becomes an example.

When your consistency becomes a signal.

When your growth becomes visible.

You do not have to force your light.

You just have to stop hiding it.

Reflect and Run

Where in my life
am I holding back
what I know I should be living out?

What would it look like
for me to show up more fully
and consistently
in who I am becoming?

Who around me
needs to see the light
I have been hesitant to reveal?

Pause.

Get honest.

Then take your next on purpose step.

Impact.

IMPACT: IT DOES NOT STOP WITH YOU

What God has done in you
was never meant to end with you.

Your growth is not just personal.

Your progress is not just for you.

Your story is not just something you survived.

It is something that can serve.

There is a pattern you will begin to notice
as you continue to grow.

The areas where you struggled the most
often become the places
you are called to serve the most.

You are often called to help
the person you once were.

The version of you
that felt overlooked
that felt uncertain
that felt like you did not belong

That is not wasted.

That is not random.

That is preparation.

Because the things you have gone through
give you language.

They give you perspective.

They give you connection.

You can speak to someone
not just from knowledge
but from experience.

There were things in my life
that I did not choose.

Pain.
Loss.
Insecurity.
Moments where I questioned my own worth.

I could not control what I was given.

But I had to take responsibility
for what I did with it.

Because what happens to you
is not always in your control.

But how you respond to it
will shape your direction.

There were people who saw something in me
before I saw it in myself.

They called me a diamond in the rough.

At the time, I did not fully understand it.

But they were right.

The potential was already inside me.

What I needed was the process
that would bring it out.

The pressure.
The challenge.

The expectations of people
who cared enough to push me.

That is what began to refine me.

Not to change who I was.

But to reveal who I was
always designed to be.

I may have been a diamond in the rough.

But a diamond sure enough.

And the same is true for you.

What you have been through
is not just something you survived.

It is something that shaped you.

Refined you.

Strengthened you.

Surviving proves you made it.

But thriving shows what the process produced.

Thriving means you did not just endure it.

You were developed by it.

You were refined by it.

That is what gives people hope.

Not just that it can be survived.

But that it can be used.

When you finish your race
you do not just complete something for yourself.

You carry something for others.

Your endurance becomes an example.

Your faithfulness becomes a model.

Your story becomes a bridge.

A bridge from where you were
to where someone else is trying to go.

In a relay race
no runner carries the baton the entire way.

Each runner prepares.

Each runner runs their portion.

But the race is not won by holding on.

It is won by passing it forward.

What has been given to you
is not meant to stop with you.

It is meant to move through you.

What flows through you
is what multiplies beyond you.

Think about a river.

A river stays fresh because it flows.

But when water is trapped
it stagnates.

The difference is not the source.

The difference is the flow.

Your life works the same way.

When what is poured into you
flows through you
it creates impact.

But when everything stops with you
it limits what your life can produce.

Many people hide the very thing
God wants to use.

They hide their past.
They hide their struggle.
They hide their process.

But often
it is the very thing
that qualifies them.

Impact is not built on perfection.

It is built on authenticity.

You do not have to have everything figured out
to make a difference.

You just have to be willing
to let what you have learned
flow through you.

That is service.

Your life carries something.

Your experiences.
Your lessons.
Your growth.

None of it is meant to stop with you.

Every step you take
creates a pathway for someone else.

This is what it means to run.

Run is not just movement.

Run is purpose in motion.

This is how you win.

Winning is not just personal.

Winning multiplies.

And this is what creates impact.

Reflect and Run

What have I gone through
that I have been hesitant to share?

Who is the person I once was
that I may be called to help now?

What would it look like
to use my story to serve someone else?

Pause.

Get honest.

Then take your next step on purpose.

Impact.

IMPACT: Own Your Race

There are things in life
that are not your fault.

What happened to you.
What you were exposed to.
What you did not have access to.
What you were not taught.

You did not choose all of it.

But you are still responsible
for what you do with it.

There was a point in my life
where I had to face this personally.

I was behind.

Behind in reading.
Behind in development.
Behind in areas that other people
seemed to move through more naturally.

And it showed.

I had to spend time
doing what others were not doing.

While others were moving forward,
I had to slow down.

I had to sit with mentors and teachers
who were willing to help me.

I had to read words
out of the dictionary.

Over and over again.

Learning them.
Pronouncing them.
Understanding them.

It was not convenient.

It was not comfortable.

But it was necessary.

The same was true
with my speech.

People laughed at me.

They made comments.

They noticed what I struggled with.

And for a moment,
I had a choice.

Let that define me.

Or decide
that it would not stop me.

I had to talk to myself.

I had to tell myself,
forget what they are saying.

I had to slow down my thoughts.

Slow down my speech.

And keep going anyway.

There were moments
I had to speak things
before I fully believed them.

I had to remind myself:

God did not make any junk.
I am His workmanship.
He has a plan for my life.
His thoughts toward me
are thoughts of peace, not evil,
to give me a future and a hope.

I did not always feel it.

But I kept saying it.

I spoke it
until it became real to me.

That was part of the process.

Not just working on the outside.

But working on the inside.

And in the middle of all of that,
something became clear.

It may not have been my fault.

But it was still my responsibility.

Responsibility meant
I had to do something different.

Responsibility meant
I had to put in extra time.

Responsibility meant
I had to grow beyond
what I was given.

And I also learned something else.

You can learn something good from people.

And you can learn something
from what not to do.

I made up my mind
that there were things
I was not going to repeat.

Cycles I was not going to continue.

Patterns I was not going to carry forward.

Not because I was better.

But because I was responsible.

That is where many people get stuck.

They spend so much time
looking backward
that they never take control
moving forward.

They focus on what was done.

What was missing.

What was unfair.

And while those things may be real,
they cannot become the reason
you stay where you are.

At some point,
responsibility becomes
the turning point.

It may not be my fault,
but it is my responsibility.

That statement shifts everything.

It removes excuses.

It removes blame.

It removes delay.

And it places you back in position.

Not in control of everything.

But in control of your response.

As it says in the Bible, Galatians 6:5:

For each one should carry their own load.

There is a difference
between what you carry
and what you were given.

You may not have chosen
what you were given.

But you are still responsible
for how you carry it.

Two people can experience
the same situation
and move in completely different directions.

One stays stuck.

One moves forward.

One blames.

One builds.

The difference is not what happened.

The difference is
what they chose to do next.

Think about it this way.

The same sun
that melts butter
hardens clay.

The sun does not change.

The environment does not change.

The difference
is in what it is applied to.

The response
determines the outcome.

Life works the same way.

The same pressure
that comes into your life
can either make you bitter
or better.

The difference
is what is happening
on the inside.

How you respond.

How you deal with it.

How you take ownership of it.

That decision
becomes the pivot.

Because responsibility
does not wait
for ideal conditions.

It moves with what is available.

It builds with what is present.

It takes ownership
of the next step.

Responsibility is not about shame.

It is about ownership.

It is not about blaming yourself.

It is about positioning yourself.

Because when you take responsibility,
you gain power.

Not power over everything.

But power over your direction.

Power over your decisions.

Power over your response.

And that is enough
to move forward.

This is where Steps On Purpose becomes real.

Because purpose
is not just discovered.

It is owned.

You cannot fully walk in
what you will not take responsibility for.

Every step you take
must be taken with ownership.

Not hesitation.

Not excuse.

Not delay.

Ownership is what turns
intention into action.

Every step you take
is either aligning you
or drifting you.

Many people wait
for clarity before they move.

They wait for confidence.

They wait for certainty.

They wait for the right conditions.

But responsibility does not wait.

It acts.

It chooses.

It steps forward
even when everything is not clear.

You do not have to have
everything figured out.

You have to take ownership
of what is in front of you.

That is how progress begins.

One decision.

One step.

One moment of ownership
at a time.

Responsibility also means
being honest.

Honest about where you are.

Honest about what needs to change.

Honest about what you have been avoiding.

Because you cannot change
what you will not face.

And you cannot move forward
if you refuse to acknowledge
where you are.

Ownership requires truth.

Real truth.

The kind that reveals
what needs to shift.

The kind that exposes
what needs to grow.

The kind that challenges you
to move differently.

And when you embrace that,
everything begins to change.

You stop waiting.

You stop blaming.

You stop delaying.

You start building.

You start moving.

You start taking control
of your direction.

You may not control
everything that happens.

But you control
what you do next.

And that is where
your power is.

This is what it means to run.

Run is not reacting.

Run is taking ownership
of your next step.

This is how you win.

Winning is not about circumstances.

Winning is about responsibility.

Winning is choosing
to move forward,
regardless of what happened
behind you.

And this is what creates impact.

Because when you take ownership
of your life,
you become someone
others can learn from.

Someone others can follow.

Someone others can be strengthened by.

Ownership is the moment
you stop explaining your position
and start changing it.

No one can run your race for you.

But no one can stop you
from owning it either.

Reflect and Run

Where am I still holding on
to what happened
instead of taking ownership
of what is next?

What responsibility
have I been avoiding
that I know I need to face?

What is the next on purpose step
I need to take
that moves me forward,
regardless of how I feel?

Pause.

Get honest.

Then take your next on purpose step.

Impact.

IMPACT: Finish Your Race

Starting is exciting.

There is energy.
There is vision.
There is momentum.

But finishing is different.

Finishing requires endurance.

It requires commitment when the excitement fades.
It requires focus when distractions increase.
It requires consistency when progress feels slow.

A lot of people start.

Few people finish.

Not because they lack ability.

But because they lose endurance along the way.

As it says in the Bible, 2 Timothy 4:7:

I have fought the good fight.
I have finished the race.
I have kept the faith.

Finishing is not about perfection.

It is about persistence.

It is about continuing when things do not go as planned.
It is about staying committed when it gets difficult.
It is about refusing to quit when it would be easier to walk away.

Finishing is not proven in one moment.

It is proven in the moments where you choose to keep going.

When the process feels longer than expected.
When the goal feels farther away than when you started.
When the weight of consistency sets in.

That is where finishing is formed.

In your life, there will be moments where the process feels longer than expected.

Where the goal feels farther away than when you started.

Where the weight of staying consistent feels heavier than the excitement of beginning.

That is where finishing is decided.

Not at the start.

But in the middle.

In the moments when no one is watching.
In the moments when progress feels invisible.
In the moments when quitting feels justified.

Finishing is a decision you make repeatedly.

Not once.

But over and over again.

You choose to keep going.
You choose to stay aligned.
You choose to follow through.

Many people fall short not because they could not finish.

But because they stopped too soon.

They got discouraged.
They got distracted.
They got tired.

And instead of adjusting, they abandoned the race.

But finishing requires you to adjust without quitting.

To slow down without stopping.
To rest without walking away.

You may not always move at the same pace.

But you can keep moving.

That is the difference.

You do not have to be the fastest.

You have to be the one who stays.

Because over time, consistency wins.
Endurance wins.
Faithfulness wins.

And those who stay in the race long enough eventually cross the finish line.

Pain is not just something you survive.

It is something that shapes you.
It refines you.
It strengthens you.

If you stay with the process, it begins to serve a purpose greater than the moment you are in.

What once felt like a setback becomes preparation.
What once felt like a struggle becomes strength.
What once felt like something you wanted to avoid becomes something that equipped you.

That is how pain becomes purpose.

Not because the pain was easy.

But because you stayed long enough to grow through it.

Every step you take
is either aligning you
or drifting you.

When you finish your race, you do not just complete something for yourself.

You carry something for others.

Your endurance becomes an example.
Your faithfulness becomes a model.
Your story becomes a bridge for someone else to keep going.

That is the impact of finishing.

This is what it means to run.

Run is not just about starting strong.

Run is about finishing what you were given to run.

This is how you win.

Winning is not about speed.

Winning is about staying.

Winning is about enduring long enough to fulfill what was placed in you.

And this is what creates impact.

Impact is not just what you start.

It is what you finish.

It is what you carry through.

It is what you release into the lives of others because you refused to quit.

Finishing is not about speed.

It is about staying.

Those who finish are the ones who refuse to quit when it matters most.

This is your race.

Not someone else's.

Not a comparison.

Not a copy.

Your race.

Marked out for you.
Set before you.
Designed with purpose.

You have come too far to stop now.

You have grown too much to go back.

You have carried too much to quit.

Stay in your lane.

Stay aligned.

Stay in motion.

Run.

Win.

Impact.

Reflect and Run

Where in my life am I tempted to stop before I finish?

What is currently testing my ability to stay committed?

What is the next on purpose step I need to take to keep moving forward, even if the pace changes?

Pause.

Get honest.

Then take your next on purpose step.

Finish your race.

IMPACT: Use Your Voice

The place you struggled most
may be the place you are called to speak from
to impact others.

There are parts of your story
that are difficult to talk about.

Moments that were painful.
Experiences that left a mark.
Seasons that shaped you
in ways you did not expect.

It is often easier to move past those moments.

To stay quiet.
To avoid the conversation.
To leave those parts of your story behind.

But your story matters.

Not just the good parts.

Not just the wins.

All of it.

Because what you have been through
carries weight.

It carries lessons.
It carries perspective.
It carries understanding.

And those things have value.

There are people
who are facing what you have already been through.

There are people
who are trying to navigate
what you have already experienced.

And what you have learned
can help them.

There was a time
when what you went through
felt like it had no purpose.

It was just difficult.

Just confusing.
Just something you had to survive.

You did not see how it could be used.

You did not see how it could help anyone else.

You just knew it was something
you had to get through.

But over time, something changed.

What once felt like pain
became perspective.

What once felt like confusion
became clarity.

What once felt like something to hide
became something you could speak from.

That is how purpose works.

It does not always show up in the moment.

Sometimes it reveals itself over time.

This is where your pain finds purpose.

Not in staying hidden.

But in being used.

This does not mean
you have to share everything with everyone.

It means you have to be willing
to use what you have been given.

You are not responsible
for telling everything.

But you are responsible
for not burying
what could help someone else.

There is a difference
between hiding and healing.

Healing allows you to move forward.

Hiding keeps you stuck.

Healing gives you language.

Hiding keeps you silent.

When you process
what you have been through,
it changes how you see it.

It is no longer just something
that happened to you.

It becomes something
you can speak from.

Something you can use.

Something that can impact others.

Your voice matters.

Not because your story is perfect.

But because it is real.

Authenticity connects.

People do not need perfection.

They need honesty.
They need truth.
They need someone who understands.

This is what your story provides.

When you speak
from what you have been through,
you give others permission.

Permission to grow.

Permission to heal.

Permission to move forward.

This is how impact happens.

Not just through what you know.

But through what you have lived.

This is where Steps On Purpose multiplies.

Because what you walked through
becomes what someone else
can walk out of.

You do not have to have all the answers.

You just have to be willing
to share what you have learned.

That is where your voice carries power.

Every step you take
is either aligning you
or drifting you.

The place you struggled most
may be the place you are called to speak from
to impact others.

Your pain was not wasted.

It was preparation.

And often,
you are called to help
the person you once were.

To speak to the version of you
that needed guidance.

To reach back
and offer what you did not have
at the time.

That is where your story
becomes a bridge.

A bridge from where you were
to where someone else is trying to go.

This is what it means to run.

Run is not just about moving forward.

Run is about carrying something
that can help someone else.

This is how you win.

Winning is not just what you achieve.

It is what you share.

It is what you give.

It is how your life
becomes useful beyond you.

This is what creates impact.

Impact is not just what you overcome.

It is what you offer
because you overcame it.

Reflect and Run

What part of my story
have I been holding back
that may be meant to help someone else?

What have I learned
through my experiences
that I have not fully acknowledged?

Who is the person I once was
that I am now called to help?

Pause.

Get honest.

Then take your next on purpose step.

Impact.

IMPACT: Finish Well

Finishing well is not about reaching the end.

It is about how you arrive there.

It is about who you have become.

What you have carried.

What you have built.

And what you leave behind.

Anyone can start.

Many can continue.

But finishing well requires intention.

It requires you to stay aligned
when distractions increase.

To stay committed
when progress feels slow.

To stay faithful
when the outcome is not immediate.

Finishing well is not built in one moment.

It is built in the daily decisions
to keep going.

To keep showing up.

To keep choosing purpose.

To keep walking in alignment
even when it would be easier to drift.

There will be moments
when the race feels longer than expected.

Moments when the weight feels heavier
than when you started.

Moments when quitting
feels reasonable.

But finishing well means
you do not stop there.

You adjust.

You refocus.

You keep moving.

Not perfectly.

But consistently.

Because finishing well
is not about speed.

It is about staying.

Over time, something happens
when you stay.

What once felt difficult
becomes discipline.

What once felt uncertain
becomes clarity.

What once felt heavy
becomes strength.

And what once felt like a struggle
becomes part of your story.

A story that someone else
will need.

A story that someone else
will learn from.

A story that becomes a bridge
between where you were
and where they are trying to go.

This is the power of finishing.

When you finish your race,
you do not just complete something for yourself.

You leave something for others.

You leave an example.

You leave a standard.

You leave a path.

Finishing well means
you ran with purpose,
you stayed aligned,
and you carried something
that made a difference.

And at the end of it all,
that is what matters.

Not how fast you moved.

Not how you compared.

Not how many times you struggled.

But that you stayed.

That you finished.

That you were faithful
to what was placed inside of you.

FINAL CHARGE

This is your race.

No one else can run it for you.

No one else can live it for you.

No one else can finish it for you.

You have been given something.

A purpose.

A direction.

An assignment.

And now, you have a choice.

Will you drift?

Or will you move with intention?

Will you react?

Or will you align?

Will you start strong
but fade away?

Or will you stay in your lane
and finish what you were given to run?

Run with purpose.

Win through faithfulness.

Impact the world around you.

One step at a time.

Stay in your lane.

Stay aligned.

Stay committed.

And whatever you do,

Finish.

IMPACT: The Commission

You did not come this far just to grow.

You did not do the work,
face the truth,
confront the gaps,
and realign your life
just for personal improvement.

This was always about more.

Everything you have walked through
has been shaping you.

Every decision.
Every stretch.
Every uncomfortable moment.

Not just for who you are becoming.

But for who your life is meant to reach.

Run. Win. Impact.

That was never just a phrase.

It is a progression.

You run by moving forward
instead of staying stuck.

You win by living aligned,
not rushed.

You impact when your growth
begins to serve someone beyond you.

Impact is where purpose
leaves your life
and enters the world around you.

As it says in the Bible, Matthew 28:19:

Go.

That word does not wait for perfection.

It does not wait for everything
to feel comfortable or clear.

Go means move with what you have.

Go means trust develops
while you are in motion.

You will not always feel ready.

Readiness is not the requirement.

Willingness is.

Purpose does not unfold all at once.

It unfolds step by step.

Clarity almost always shows up
after movement, not before it.

There are people connected
to your obedience.

People who benefit
when you stop overthinking
and start stepping.

People who need
what you have learned,
lived, and survived.

That is why Steps On Purpose exists.

Because movement without intention
leads to burnout.

And intention without movement
leads to frustration.

Before every meaningful step,
there is a moment.

A moment to pause.
A moment to realign.
A moment to check direction.

In Scripture,
that moment is called Selah.

Selah is the pause
that brings clarity.

Selah is where you get honest
about where you are.

Selah is where you remember
why you started.

But Selah is not where you live.

It is where you prepare
to move forward the right way.

So take a Selah Step.

Pause long enough
to tell yourself the truth.

Where are you right now?

What have you been avoiding?

What is your next on purpose step?

Then take it.

Not ten steps.

Not perfect steps.

Just the next aligned one.

Purpose is not lived in giant leaps.

It is lived in intentional steps
taken consistently.

The step you take today
can shift your direction.

The step you take today
can open a door for someone else.

The step you take today
can become the foundation
for something that lasts beyond you.

That is impact.

Your life is not small.

Your story is not insignificant.

Your purpose is not random.

You were designed.

You were called.

You were equipped.

Now go.

Run your race with intention.

Win by staying aligned.

Impact lives that are not just yours.

Pause when you need to.

Realign when you drift.

But do not stay stuck.

Take a Selah Step.

Pause.

Get honest.

Then move on purpose.

And go.

A FINAL WORD

Before you move forward, pause.

Not to stop.

But to recognize.

Look at how far you have come.

Look at what you have faced.

Look at what you have grown through.

You are not the same person
who started this journey.

Something has shifted.

Something has developed.

Something has become clearer.

You see differently.

You think differently.

You move differently.

And that matters.

Because this was never just about information.

It was about transformation.

Not just learning something new.

But becoming someone new.

You have been reminded
that your life has purpose.

That your steps matter.

That your direction is not random.

You have seen
what it means to run with intention.

To win through alignment.

To impact beyond yourself.

Now it belongs to you.

No one can take your steps for you.

No one can make your decisions for you.

No one can live this out in your place.

But you are not starting from nothing.

You have clarity.

You have awareness.

You have direction.

And that is enough
to take the next step.

You do not need everything figured out.

You just need to keep moving
with purpose in every step.

So as you go forward, remember this:

Stay aligned.

Stay aware.

Stay intentional.

And whatever you do,

Do not drift.

You were not created to wander.

You were created to move with purpose.

This is your race.

Own it.

Walk it.

Live it.

One step at a time.

Key Concepts and Framework Guide

This section is designed to help you revisit the core ideas, language, and principles from this book.

These are not just definitions.

They are anchors.
They are reminders.
They are tools you can return to
as you continue to run your race with purpose.

They shape how you think.
They guide how you live.
They influence how you lead yourself
and others forward.

Design

The truth that your life was intentional before it was visible.
Before you ever made a decision, there was already a design.

Identity

Who you are is not built on performance, but rooted in how you were created and known.
You are not becoming someone new.
You are becoming who you were designed to be.

Worth

Your value is not something you earn.
It is something you live from.
You do not perform to earn worth.
You live from the worth already given.

Grace

The foundation that establishes your worth before you achieve anything.
Grace shifts you from striving to becoming.

Direction

The path your daily decisions are shaping over time.
What you consistently allow will eventually determine your direction.

Discipline

The commitment to stay consistent regardless of how you feel.
Discipline carries you when motivation runs out.

Environment

The influences, people, and inputs that are shaping your thinking and behavior.
What is shaping you is steering you.

Ownership

Taking responsibility for your life, regardless of what you did not choose.
It may not be your fault, but it is still your responsibility.

Pain

Difficult experiences that, when processed, can become a source of strength and growth.
Pain does not have to break you.
It can build what purpose requires.

Voice

The ability to use your story, experiences, and lessons to impact others.
The place you struggled most may be the place you are called to speak from to impact others.

Service

Using what you have been given to benefit others beyond yourself.
What God pours into you was never meant to stop with you.

Finish

The commitment to remain faithful over time.
Finishing well is not about perfection.
It is about faithfulness.

Run™

Living with intentional movement and forward progress.
You are not standing still.
Every step is shaping your direction.

Win™

Faithfulness in alignment with your purpose, even when it is not visible.
If you are still running, you are still winning.

Impact™

The influence your life has on others when you live with purpose.
Your life was never meant to stop with you.

The Designer Lens™

Seeing yourself and others based on how God created them, not just their performance or past.
When you see through The Designer Lens™, you recognize potential before it is visible.

Alignment

Living in agreement with your design, purpose, and direction.
Alignment keeps you moving toward what you were created to do.

Faithfulness

Consistency over time, regardless of feelings or circumstances.
Faithfulness is what carries you to the finish.

Next Step

The immediate action in front of you that moves you forward.
You do not need the whole path.
You need the next step.

The Selah Step™

A moment to pause, get honest, and realign before moving forward.
You do not pause to stay still.
You pause so you can move forward the right way.

Run Win Impact™ Framework

A simple way to understand how purpose is lived out daily.

Run with intention.
Win through faithfulness.
Impact others through how you live.

This is not a theory.
This is how purpose is practiced daily.

Core Principle

Everything in this book comes back to this:

Run with purpose.
Win through faithfulness.
Impact the world around you.

Run™, Win™, Impact™, The Designer Lens™, The Selah Step™, and the Run Win Impact™ Framework are part of the Steps On Purpose™ ecosystem.

CREED

RUN WIN IMPACT

I was designed with purpose.

I am not accidental.
I am intentional.

I am called to run my course.

I will stay in my lane.
I will move with direction.

I am built to win through faithfulness.

Not by comparison,
but by alignment.

I trust the One who leads me.

I am not carrying this alone.

What God started in me,
He will complete.

I will stay in the race.

I will not quit when it is hard.
I will not ease up when it matters most.

I will find my kick.

I will keep going.
I will increase focus.
I will commit fully.

I will finish with what I have left.

I will finish strong.

I will run through the line,
not to it, but through it.

My life is not just for me.

What I carry is meant to flow through me.

What flows through me
will impact others.

I am created to make an impact.

I will serve.
I will influence.
I will make a difference.

I am not chasing purpose.

I am walking it out,
one intentional step at a time.

Run.
Win.
Impact.

FRAMEWORK

RUN WIN IMPACT

A simple framework for living with purpose every day.

RUN™ — HOW YOU LIVE

Identity — Know who you are
Direction — Stay aligned with purpose
Discipline — Take consistent steps
Endurance — Keep going when it gets hard

Run is intentional movement.

You are not drifting.
You are moving forward with purpose.

WIN™ — HOW YOU MEASURE SUCCESS

Faithfulness — Stay committed
Obedience — Follow what is right
Alignment — Stay true to your calling

Winning is not about being ahead of others.

Winning is staying aligned
with what God has called you to do.

IMPACT™ — HOW YOU MAKE A DIFFERENCE

Service — Give what you have
Influence — Affect others positively
Multiplication — What flows through you reaches others

Impact is not measured by attention.

It is measured by transformation.

THE SELAH STEP™ — HOW YOU REALIGN

Pause — Stop long enough to see clearly
Examine — Get honest about where you are
Listen — Reconnect to truth and direction
Act — Take your next on purpose step

You

KEY SCRIPTURES

These Scriptures anchor the principles of Run Win Impact.

Return to them often.
Reflect on them deeply.
Live them daily.

Hebrews 12:1–2

"Therefore, since we are surrounded by such a great cloud of witnesses, let us throw off everything that hinders and the sin that so easily entangles. And let us run with perseverance the race marked out for us, fixing our eyes on Jesus, the author and finisher of our faith."

A call to run with endurance, stay focused, and trust Jesus as both the starting point and the One who completes your journey.

Galatians 5:7

"You were running well. Who hindered you from obeying the truth?"

A reminder to stay aligned with truth and not allow distractions, pressure, or comparison to pull you off course.

Philippians 1:6

"Being confident of this, that He who began a good work in you will carry it on to completion until the day of Christ Jesus."

A reminder that your journey is not dependent on you alone. God is faithful to complete what He started in you.

2 Timothy 4:7

“I have fought the good fight, I have finished the race, I have kept the faith.”

A picture of what it means to finish well. Not perfect, but faithful.

Matthew 28:19

“Go and make disciples of all nations...”

A call to move, to act, and to let your life impact others beyond yourself.

Galatians 6:9

“Let us not become weary in doing good, for at the proper time we will reap a harvest if we do not give up.”

A reminder that consistency matters. Keep going, even when results are not immediate.

Proverbs 3:5–6

“Trust in the Lord with all your heart and lean not on your own understanding; in all your ways submit to Him, and He will make your paths straight.”

A reminder to trust God’s direction, even when the path is not fully clear.

Core Reminder

Run with purpose.
Win through faithfulness.
Impact the world around you.

GROUP DISCUSSION GUIDE

RUN WIN IMPACT

Use this guide to reflect, discuss, and apply the principles from each section of the book.

Be honest.
Be open.
Focus on growth, not perfection.

SESSION 1 — RUN™ (Identity and Direction)

What stood out most to you in this section?

Where do you feel most aligned with your purpose right now?

Where do you feel misaligned or unsure?

What is one intentional next step you need to take to move forward?

SESSION 2 — DISCIPLINE AND ENDURANCE

Where do you struggle most to stay consistent?

What is currently testing your endurance?

What distractions or habits are pulling you off course?

What is one way you can stay in motion this week?

SESSION 3 — WIN™ (Faithfulness)

How do you define winning at this stage of your life?

Where have you been measuring success incorrectly?

What does faithfulness look like in your daily life?

Where do you need to stay committed, even when it is not visible?

SESSION 4 — IMPACT™ (Service and Influence)

Who has had a significant impact on your life, and why?

Where do you currently have opportunities to serve others?

What has been placed in you that could benefit someone else?

What is one intentional way you can make a difference this week?

SESSION 5 — FINISHING (KICK)

Where are you most tempted to ease up or quit?

What does your KICK look like in this season?

Keep going
Increase focus
Commit fully
Kick with what is left

What would it mean for you to finish strong in this area?

SESSION 6 — THE COMMISSION

What are you being called to do next?

What is one clear commitment you are making moving forward?

How will you live Run • Win • Impact on a daily basis?

Who can help hold you accountable to what you committed?

CLOSE EACH SESSION

Identify one next step.
Commit to it.
Take action.

Pause.

Get honest.

Then take the next step on purpose.

REFLECT & RUN

Use these questions to slow down, get honest, and take your next step on purpose.

What would your future self thank you for choosing today?

Where am I currently out of alignment?

What step do I need to take right now?

What am I avoiding that I need to face?

What is one area where I need to stay consistent?

Where am I tempted to quit too early?

What does faithfulness look like in this season?

Who can benefit from what I have been through?

Where can I make an impact this week?

What is my next intentional step?

Pause.

Get honest.

Then take your next step on purpose.

PUTTING IT INTO PRACTICE

Pause.
Get honest.
Then take the next step on purpose.

ONE FOCUS AREA

What is one area I will focus on right now?

ONE NEXT STEP

What is the next step I will take?

ONE PERSON TO IMPACT

Who can I serve or support?

ONE COMMITMENT

What will I stay consistent with?

FINAL REMINDER

Stay in your lane.
Stay in motion.
Stay aligned.

Run.
Win.
Impact.

SIGNATURE QUOTES

RUN WIN IMPACT

YOU ARE DESIGNED

You are not chasing purpose.
You are walking it out.

You were created on purpose,
with purpose,
for purpose.

Before you ever made a decision,
there was already a design.

RUN — HOW YOU LIVE

Run with purpose, not pressure.

You do not drift into purpose.
You decide into it.

Direction matters more than speed.

Stay in your lane.
Stay in motion.
Stay aligned.

You are not standing still.
Every step is shaping your direction.

STAY IN THE RACE

You do not have to be perfect to stay in the race.
You have to be consistent.

The race is not won by those who never struggle.
It is won by those who keep running.

You were running well.
What pulled you off course?

If you are still running in alignment,
you are still winning.

WIN — HOW YOU MEASURE SUCCESS

Winning is not about being ahead of others.

Winning is staying aligned
with what you were called to do.

Faithfulness is the real measure of success.

Consistency over time
creates the life you are called to live.

TRUST THE LEADER

You need more confidence in God's ability to lead you
than in your ability to follow Him.

It will not be because you were a perfect follower,
but because God is a faithful Leader.

What God started in you,
He will complete.

Grace is not what you fall back on.
It is what you have been standing in all along.

KICK — HOW YOU FINISH

The last stretch is where you lock in.

Find your KICK
and run through the line.

Do not slow down
in the stretch that matters most.

Finish strong.
Finish aligned.
Finish faithful.

IMPACT — HOW YOU MAKE A DIFFERENCE

Impact is not measured by attention.

It is measured by transformation.

What you carry
is not meant to stop with you.

What flows through you
is what multiplies beyond you.

Your life is not just about you.
It is meant to serve others.

VOICE AND PURPOSE

Your pain has a voice.
Your story has value.

What you walked through
can help someone else walk out.

The place you struggled most
may be the place you are called to speak from.

THE SELAH STEP

Pause long enough to see clearly.

Get honest about where you are.

Realignment happens in moments,
not just milestones.

You do not pause to stay still.
You pause so you can move forward the right way.

Clarity grows
when you are willing to face the truth.

You do not need the whole path.
You need the next step.

Take a Selah Step.
Pause. Get honest. Then move on purpose.

THE DIAMOND

You may have been a diamond in the rough,
but a diamond sure enough.

The value was always there.

The process did not create you.
It revealed you.

Pressure did not break you.
It refined you.

FINAL CHARGE

You were not created just to start.
You were created to finish.

Run your race.
Win through faithfulness.
Impact the world around you.

Pause when you need to.
Realign when you drift.
But do not stay stuck.

Take the next step on purpose.

Run.
Win.
Impact.

This is Your Race.

Run it with purpose.

Win through faithfulness.

And finish it well.

Run.

Win.

Impact.

www.ingramcontent.com/pod-product-compliance
Lightning Source LLC
Chambersburg PA
CBHW030936060726
47591CB00005B/1824
9781972165027